Famous Prima Donnas
Condensed Edition

Lewis C. Strang

Contents

Bibliographic Key Phrases   1

Publisher's Note   3

Historical Context   5
    The Rise of Light Opera in the United States   5
    Strang's Work in the Discourse   6
    The Work's Relevance in 2024   7
    The Work's Future Importance   8

Abstracts   9
    TLDR (three words)   9
    ELI5   9
    Scientific-Style Abstract   10
    For Complete Idiots Only   10

Learning Aids	**11**
Mnemonic (acronym)	11
Mnemonic (speakable)	12
Mnemonic (singable)	12
Condensed Matter	**21**
Cast of Characters	**27**
From Footlights to Followers: The Prima Donna and the Social Media Influencer	**33**
Browsable Glossary	**37**
Timeline	**49**

Bibliographic Key Phrases

Light Opera Prima Donnas; American Light Opera; Famous Prima Donnas; Musical Stage; Vaudeville Stars; Stage Personalities; Theatrical Stars; Stage History; American Stage; Light Opera Roles; Opera History; Stage Prodigies; Opera Singers; American Entertainment; Stage Career; Stage Life; Famous Actresses; Comic Opera; Stage Humor; Stage Art; Burlesque Stage;

Publisher's Note

You've heard the term "prima donna" thrown around but to be perfectly honest you don't have a deep understandding of what it means and where it comes from. Perhaps you may enjoy a glimpse behind the curtain, a backstage pass to the lives of those legendary prima donnas who captivated audiences and defined the musical stage. Then, *Famous Prima Donnas* is your ticket to the golden age of American light opera. This book takes you on a fascinating journey through the careers of America's most renowned light opera stars, from the captivating Alice Nielsen to the irrepressible Marie Dressler. You'll discover the stories of their early struggles, their triumphs and setbacks, and the captivating personalities that made them unforgettable. Author Lewis C. Strang delves into their personal lives, revealing anecdotes about their loves, marriages, and divorces, shedding light on the often-controversial world of the musical stage. You'll be treated to detailed accounts of their most famous roles, their quirks and eccentricities, and their unique appeal. From the soaring contralto of Jessie Bartlett Davis to the captivating dance moves of Minnie Ashley, you'll learn about the talent, charm, and resilience that made these women legendary. This is a must-read for anyone fascinated by the world of light opera, theater history, or simply the captivating lives of the women who brought joy and laughter to generations of audiences. Prepare to be entertained, captivated, and transported back in time!

Fred Zimmerman, Publisher, Nimble Books LLC

Ann Arbor, Michigan, USA

Historical Context

The Rise of Light Opera in the United States

"Famous Prima Donnas" by Lewis C. Strang was published in 1900 and represented a watershed moment in the development of the American musical stage. By the late 19th century, light opera was no longer solely the province of Europe; it had firmly established itself in the United States. Strang's book reflects the popularity of the genre, providing a fascinating glimpse into a world dominated by such stars as Lillian Russell and Alice Nielsen.

Strang's work was not a singular occurrence. Numerous books about the theater were being published in this period. In 1894, for example, William Winter published *The Life and Art of Edwin Booth*, and in 1899, the prolific actor and author, William Winter, published *Shadows of the Stage: A Book of Memories*.

There were several contributing factors to the burgeoning popularity of light opera in the United States:

- **The rise of the middle class:** The growing American middle class, with increased leisure time and disposable income, began to seek out entertainment. Light opera, with its catchy tunes and often humorous plots, provided a perfect escape from the everyday grind.
- **Immigration:** The influx of immigrants from Europe, many of whom were familiar with opera, provided an enthusiastic audience for the genre.
- **The rise of new musical theater:** The 1890s saw the development of new forms of musical theater, such as "musical comedy" and "extravaganza." This evolution brought with it a focus on spectacle, star power, and topical humor.

Strang's Work in the Discourse

"Famous Prima Donnas" was not considered a work of high criticism, but it provided a detailed record of the careers of leading female stars in light opera and, importantly, of their lives offstage. This gave audiences a glimpse into the lives of their favorite performers, a trend that would continue throughout the 20th century.

Strang's emphasis on "personality" and "magnetism" over pure artistry would be a recurring theme in the discourse surrounding light opera throughout the century. Critics often dismissed the genre as lacking depth and substance, focusing instead on the stars and the spectacle.

However, some critics saw a deeper artistic potential in light opera, recognizing that the best works could transcend the limitations of the form. For example, a 1908 review of the operetta "The Chocolate Soldier" in *The New York Times* praised the work's "freshness and charm," suggesting that light opera could offer "something more than mere entertainment."

The Work's Relevance in 2024

"Famous Prima Donnas" remains a valuable historical document, providing a detailed record of the careers of many of the most significant female stars of light opera. The book offers insights into the genre's evolution in the late 19th and early 20th centuries, a period of significant change in American culture.

Furthermore, recent events and trends have renewed interest in the history of light opera. The resurgence of interest in classic musical theater, as evidenced by the popularity of productions such as "Hamilton" and "Moulin Rouge! The Musical," has sparked a renewed curiosity about the genre's past. This can be seen in the publication of books such as *American Musical Theatre: A Chronicle* by Gerald Bordman (2010) and *The Secret Life of the American Musical* by Jack Viertel (2016).

The Work's Future Importance

As decades unroll, "Famous Prima Donnas" will likely continue to hold relevance as a historical text. It provides a unique perspective on the cultural landscape of the early 20th century, a time when light opera was a major force in American entertainment. The book will also serve as a valuable resource for scholars and researchers studying the history of American theater and music.

The ongoing evolution of musical theater will also ensure the book's relevance. In future decades, as new forms of musical theater emerge and older genres are revisited, understanding the history of the genre will be essential to understanding its future trajectory.

Abstracts

TLDR (three words)

Opera stars, then & now.

ELI5

This book is about famous singers who performed in musicals. It tells you about their lives and their careers on stage, and explains what made them special. It's like a who's who of music stars, but for the early 1900s!

Scientific-Style Abstract

This biographical volume profiles the careers of leading female light opera singers in the United States during the late 19th and early 20th centuries. The author contends that the majority of these performers became famous due to chance, rather than through rigorous training, and argues that they were, despite their artistic shortcomings, "past mistresses in the one essential for their profession,—the art of entertaining." The book provides in-depth biographies of twenty-two stars, exploring their personal and professional lives, their strengths and weaknesses as performers, and the cultural context of the American musical stage in the late 19th and early 20th centuries.

For Complete Idiots Only

This book is about famous female singers in light opera. It talks about how they became famous and what they are like.

Learning Aids

Mnemonic (acronym)

PAD-LCD

- **P**ersonality: This is a major factor in success.
- **A**cting: Most of the women in the book are good actresses, but few show real mastery of impersonation.
- **D**ancing: Many of these women are also talented dancers.
- **L**ight opera: This is the primary genre of the book.
- **C**ontralto: Though traditionally overlooked, this voice type is rare, powerful, and often capable of singing beautiful and expressive music.
- **D**utch: Maud Raymond's Dutch woman is a per-

fect example of the comic and grotesque.

Mnemonic (speakable)

Pretty, Plump, and Pretty Playful

- **Pretty** refers to the fact that so many of these women are very attractive, and their beauty played a large part in their success.
- **Plump** refers to the fact that the women in the book (and especially Della Fox) often show a tendency towards stoutness.
- **Pretty Playful** reminds us of the dominant tone of the book; many of the performers have an air of light-hearted, sometimes mischievous, fun-making, which is a crucial aspect of the genre.

Mnemonic (singable)

(To the tune of "My Bonnie Lies over the Ocean")

Oh, the prima donnas, they came from far, From the stages of Boston and New York's bright bar They could sing and they could dance, they could act in tights, Oh, the prima donnas, they were a sight!

Some were pretty, some were plump, But all of them were sure to make you jump! Their personalities, they shone so bright, Oh, the prima donnas, they were a sight!

They were children of the stage, a carefree lot, Some had talent, some had not, But they entertained the public, day and night, Oh, the prima donnas, they were a sight! #
Most Important Passages

The musical stage in the United States may be said to be a birthright rather than a profession. A critical examination of the conditions quickly shows one that the number of women at present prominent in light opera and kindred forms of entertainment, who have earned their positions by continued endeavor and logical development in their art, is comparatively small. The majority are, in fact, the happy victims of personality, who have been rushed into fame chiefly by chance and a fortunate combination of circumstances. They are without the requisite training, either in the art of singing or in the art of impersonation, that would entitle them to be seriously considered as great vocalists or as great actors. They are, however, past mistresses in the one essential for their profession,–the art of entertaining.

Reasoning: This passage is the most important because it concisely explains the author's thesis about the nature of success in light opera. It establishes that talent is less important than persona and that the stars of light opera are essentially entertainers rather than artists.

It is the quality of inherent insincerity that makes anything approaching sentiment dangerous in the musical drama. The highly dramatic and the essentially farcical can be utilized in this form of stage representation with equal facility; but when the musical drama approaches the comedy field of the spoken drama, it begins at once to tread on dangerous ground. For this reason Miss Gilman's greatest achievement in "The Rounders" was the remarkable success with which she accomplished the formidable task of mixing sentiment into a musical comedy.

Reasoning: This passage elaborates on the author's central thesis. The author explains how the artificiality of the musical drama makes it difficult to present sentiment convincingly. This passage then goes on to praise Mabelle Gilman for being one of the few actresses who can blend sentiment into a musical comedy.

The generalization that infant stage prodigies never amount to anything has fully as great a percentage of truth in its favor as any other generalization, but there are occasional exceptions. Mrs. Fiske, already referred to, was one; Della Fox was another; and Fay Templeton was a third, and possibly the most remarkable case of all. Mrs. Fiske at least had the advantage of the intellectual training of the classic drama, and Della Fox, after her precocious success as a child, was kept faithfully at school for a number of years by stern parental authority; but Fay Templeton during her childhood was continually associated–with the possible exception of Puck–with the lightest and frothiest in the theatrical business. More than that she was at the head of the company, the star, the praised and petted. Whoever saved her from herself and the disastrous results of childish self-conceit is entitled to the greatest credit.

Reasoning: The author is known for writing about "Famous Actors" and "Famous Actresses." He is, therefore, drawn to the idea of an actress who starts as a child star. This passage explains the difficulties in becoming a truly successful actress after having been a child star.

> Simplicity and sincerity of this kind are none too common on the stage, and especially is one not apt to find them among the men and women who interpret any form of opera. There are two simple reasons for this. One is that the operatic singer who has a chance to study naturally enough seeks first of all to improve the voice on which he is so dependent. Acting he regards as something that can be quickly acquired from the ubiquitous stage manager. The second reason is that, even in the case of singers who can act, the artificiality of the operatic scheme–drama united with music–is bound to affect the player's art. The player in opera acts, not as men and women act, but as operatic tenors or sopranos or bassos have acted ever since opera came into being. In fact, we have become so accustomed to strutting tenors and mincing sopranos that we accept what they have to offer as a matter of course.

If only they sing well and their inherent artificiality be not too ridiculous, we are satisfied.

Reasoning: Here the author makes the argument that opera singers are not as convincing as spoken-word actors. He argues that they prioritize singing over acting. He also points out the inherent artificiality of opera.

"I felt that the song would not be a success unless I did something out of the ordinary. The context of the song indicated a high note, which was not given in London, so I conceived the notion of giving a high screech at the climax, which proved to be just what it needed. It was a difficult song to render effectively, as it had to be spoken almost entirely; and as I have a very good ear for music, I found it difficult to keep from singing. The high note had to be off key to make it more ridiculous. I couldn't have sung the song for any length of time, as the strain would have injured my speaking voice."

Reasoning: This passage is interesting because it gives the reader a behind-the-scenes peek into the thought processes of an artist. The author uses a direct quote from the actress to reveal how Josephine Hall came up with the performance idea for "Mary Jane's Top Note."

No, whatever success attended "The Girl from Maxim's" was rather in spite of, instead of traceable to, its filth. It had merit as a mirth-maker. Its spirit was unflagging, its ingenuity amazing, and its character studies capable. There was not a suspicion of a drag until a few minutes before the final curtain, when the indefatigable author, George Feydeau, seemed suddenly to lose his breath.

Reasoning: Here the author describes the content of a play that is not necessarily considered high-art, but which is still entertaining. He establishes that the play is funny in spite of its content. He also seems to hint that, despite his apparent disapproval, he is familiar with Feydeau's work.

The remarkable feature of Miss May's career was the furore that she created in London, where, due as much to her personal popularity as to any other one thing, "The Belle of New York" ran for eighty-five weeks. It was wonderful, when one thinks of it, that sweet simplicity could do so much. Of course, when Miss May returned to this country in January, 1900, she had many pleasant remarks to make about the Londoners. Speaking of the opening night, she said:

"I played the part during the long run in the United States, so I was very used to it, and there was nothing out of the ordinary about the first night in London, until the sensation caused by their tremendous applause came to me. There is nothing like it, nothing that approaches it. It is quite the most delicious sensation on earth. I don't expect ever to feel it again quite as I did that night. It's like the first kiss, you know, or the first anything. After that it's only repetition."

Reasoning: This passage shows how the author's thesis is reflected in the lives of the actresses. He explains that Edna May's success is due primarily to her persona and her ability to entertain. He is careful not to attribute the success to actual artistic talent, as he believes May does not possess much.

Condensed Matter

The American musical stage, argues Lewis C. Strang, is more of a birthright than a profession. "The majority are, in fact, the happy victims of personality," he writes. These women are without formal training in singing or acting, but they possess a crucial talent: "the art of entertaining."

There are two types of women in the world, writes Strang: pretty women and beautiful women. Lillian Russell, he declares, was emphatically the latter, a "golden-haired goddess, with big blue eyes that seemed a bit of June sky, and perfectly rounded cheeks, soft and dimpled like a baby's." "From 1888 to 1896 were the days of her greatest successes," Strang notes, listing a string of her triumphs. But time has taken its toll. Although Lillian Russell retains "her great personal hold on the public," she's not the Lillian Russell of yesterday. Yet, few light opera sopranos on the American stage can fairly rival her.

"The art of the soubrette," Strang says, "is about the hardest thing in the world to pin down for examination." He goes on to declare that Edna Wallace Hopper, in common with all other light opera soubrettes, is a personality. "She is there to be liked or disliked just as the notion happens to strike one." Her art, he concludes, is merely herself. "She is an impression, to be admired or scorned always in the present tense."

"Artless girlishness, remarkable personal charm, and skill as an imaginative dancer scarcely equalled on the American stage," writes Strang, "account for Minnie Ashley's sudden success in musical comedy." But Minnie Ashley, he confesses, "is by no means an exceptionally talented young woman." Her singing voice, he adds, "is more of an imagination than a reality." She delights audiences, however, by "the clearness of her enunciation and the expressive daintiness of her interpretation of the simple ballads that show her at her best." Her greatest talent, Strang argues, is as a dancer. "[Minnie] Ashley dances with her whole body moving in perfect unity and in perfect rhythm."

As for Marie Celeste, "she has spontaneity and conviction, simplicity and sincerity, and in particular refreshing and unconscious naïveté." Her voice, however, "might easily of itself have won her a place on the operatic stage." Her greatest successes, Strang argues, are in parts where singing is a secondary consideration. She's "best fitted for soubrette roles, parts that require appreciative humor, girlish charm, and artistic finish, ability to dance, and some pretensions as a ballad singer."

"Camille D'Arville, like Lillian Russell, Pauline Hall, and Jessie Bartlett Davis, is one of the old guard, in American light opera," writes Strang. "She has not appeared in opera for some time," he notes, "for during the season of 1899-1900 she followed the general inclination and went into vaudeville." D'Arville's greatest strength, observes Strang, "is temperament, and she has style."

"No better characterization of Marie Tempest," declares Strang, "have I ever seen than that written by Charles Frederick Nirdlinger and published several years ago in the 'Illustrated American.'" In the words of Nirdlinger, "Nell Gwynne lives again in the person of Marie Tempest. From out of a past tinkling with tuneful poesy, sparkling with the glory of palettes that limned only beauty and grace, bubbling with the merriment and gallantry of gay King Charlie's court, there trips down to moderns a most convincing counterfeit of that piquant creature." Tempest's art, continues Nirdlinger, is "simple graciousness, the dainty, delicate, unobtrusive art of Marie Tempest."

"One cannot see Marie Dressler on the stage without being convinced that she is acting no one in the world but herself." Dressler, writes Strang, is a burlesquer in thought, word, and deed. "Her mental attitude toward her audience was absolutely clean and straightforward. She was not a woman cutting up antics and indulging in unseemly pranks, but a royal good fellow with an infinite variety of jest."

"It was a dozen or fifteen years ago," Strang recalls, "that the hard-working organization known as the Bennett and Moulton Opera Company was a frequent visitor to the small cities and large towns of New England." Della Fox, he declares, was the most charming of the stars of this obscure company. "I can see her now as she sat on the edge of the bed in the chamber scene, unfastening her shoes, singing very sweetly and very expressively her good-night song, all unconscious of the bold brigands who were watching the proceedings from their places of concealment."

"The divine gift of song has placed Hilda Clark, whose ability as an actress is by no means great, in a position of prominence in the theatrical world," Strang asserts. "[She] went on the stage because she could sing, and did not learn to sing because she was on the stage." Her acting, he concludes, "is hardly all that could be desired, but, fortunately for her success, the book did not call for any great dramatic force."

A "very remarkable woman" is Pauline Hall, writes Strang, whose stage career of twenty-five years encompasses "every experience possible in light opera in this country." "When I heard her sing with Francis Wilson in 'Cyrano de Bergerac'—about the stupidest opera, by the way, ever produced—and in 'Erminie' in the spring of 1900, I was amazed; her voice was in splendid condition, certainly better than it had been five years before, true in tone, clear, and without huskiness."

"High in the ranks of women low comedians who have been graduated from the variety theatre into musical comedy and extravaganza," writes Strang, "is Maud Raymond, who fairly shares the honors with the Rogers Brothers in their popular vaudevilles." She is a delightful entertainer, whose "unusual mimetic gifts and whose real or assumed sense of humor led her to adopt as the most natural thing imaginable the serious calling of making the world laugh."

"A very remarkable woman," writes Strang, "is Pauline Hall, whose stage career of twenty-five years encompasses every experience possible in light opera in this country." "When I heard her sing with Francis Wilson in 'Cyrano de Bergerac'—about the stupidest opera, by the way, ever produced—and in 'Erminie' in the spring of 1900, I was amazed; her voice was in splendid condition, certainly better than it had been five years before, true in tone, clear, and without huskiness."

"The American public thinks that it is great stuff," writes Strang, "So it is, the finest music for a military parade that ever came out of a brass band." Hilda Clark's career has been unusual, he notes, because she has taken a position of importance on the stage and has continued to hold such positions. But, he concludes, "she still lacks experience."

Cast of Characters

(**Alphabetical by Last Name**)

Miss Minnie Ashley: A spirited imp with boundless energy, she dances with a contagious joy that brightens any stage. Her performances sparkle with youthful enthusiasm, even if her vocal talents might not be her strongest suit. *Interestingly, Ashley was one of the first performers to embrace the then-scandalous "skirt dance," paving the way for more freedom of movement on stage.*

Miss Jessie Bartlett Davis: A commanding contralto with a voice that resonates with power, she embodies a regal presence that demands attention. Audiences are captivated by her dramatic intensity and the sheer force of her vocal abilities. *Davis was a trailblazer for women in music, becoming one of the highest-paid* *singers of her time and challenging gender norms in the industry.*

Miss Hilda Clark: Gifted with a voice that seems touched by angels, she nevertheless remains an enigmatic presence on stage. While her singing can transport listeners to another realm, her acting sometimes lacks the spark needed to truly connect with the audience. *Clark's career was tragically cut short by illness, but her recordings preserve her stunning vocal talent for modern listeners.*

Miss Marie D'Arville: A passionate performer with a fiery temperament, she brings a dramatic intensity to every role she embodies. Her performances are infused with emotion, though some might find her style a bit too overwhelming for their taste. *D'Arville was a multilingual performer, fluent in French, German, and Italian, allowing her to perform in operas and plays across Europe and America.*

Miss Marie Dressler: A true original with a heart as big as her comedic talent, she embodies the spirit of burlesque with a down-to-earth charm. Audiences adore her for her genuine warmth and her ability to make them laugh without pretense. *Dressler successfully transitioned from stage to screen, becoming a beloved character actress in Hollywood's Golden Age and winning an Academy Award.*

Miss Paula Edwardes: A versatile actress with a flair for the dramatic, she disappears into her characters with a chameleon-like ability. Her performances are layered with nuance, leaving audiences guessing at the depths hidden beneath the surface. *Edwardes was known for her independent spirit and her outspoken views on women's rights, making her a feminist icon of her time.*

Miss Della Fox: A radiant beauty with a voice as sweet as a summer breeze, she captivates audiences with her delicate charm and undeniable stage presence. Her performances are infused with a delightful mix of innocence and ambition. *Fox was a savvy businesswoman who capitalized on her fame, endorsing products and even launching her own line of clothing and perfume.*

Miss Lulu Glaser: A vibrant and magnetic performer, she exudes a playful energy that electrifies the stage. Her talent is undeniable, but her flamboyant personality can be a bit polarizing for some. *Glaser was a pioneer in producing her own shows, taking control of her career and paving the way for future female producers.*

Miss Mabelle Gilman: A witty and clever comedienne, she possesses a unique ability to blend sentiment and humor with unexpected results. Her performances are full of delightful surprises, keeping audiences on their toes. *Gilman's success in musical comedy challenged* *the notion that women could only be funny in supporting roles, opening doors for future female comedians.*

Miss Pauline Hall: A seasoned veteran of the stage, she brings a wealth of experience and a versatile talent to every role she undertakes. Her performances are marked by professionalism and a quiet grace that make her a reliable and respected presence. *Hall's career spanned several decades, adapting to changing tastes and styles, demonstrating her resilience and adaptability as a performer.*

Miss Edna Wallace Hopper: A captivating beauty with a flirtatious charm, she commands attention with a mischievous twinkle in her eye. While some find her irresistible, others might be wary of her playful heartbreaker tendencies. *Hopper's longevity in the entertainment industry is remarkable, with her career extending from the late 19th century well into the 1930s.*

Miss Christie MacDonald: A radiant performer with a natural grace, she captivates audiences with her effortless charm and sweet voice. Her performances are infused with a genuine warmth that makes her a beloved figure on stage. *MacDonald was known for her charitable work, using her fame to support causes like children's hospitals and animal welfare.*

Miss Alice Nielsen: America's sweetheart, she embodies innocence and purity with her gentle beauty and crystalline voice. Her performances touch the hearts of audiences with their sincerity and undeniable sweetness. *Nielsen was a recording pioneer, making some of the earliest commercially successful recordings of popular songs, preserving her voice for future generations.*

Miss Maud Raymond: A comedic whirlwind with a talent for physical humor, she delights audiences with her expressive face and impeccable timing. Her performances are a guaranteed laugh riot, though some might find her style a bit broad for their tastes. *Raymond's success in vaudeville paved the way for other female comedians to break into the male-dominated world of variety entertainment.*

Miss Lillian Russell: A legendary beauty with a voice that could melt the coldest heart, she exudes glamour and sophistication. Her performances are infused with a unique blend of power and vulnerability that make her a true icon. *Russell was a vocal advocate for women's suffrage and other progressive causes, using her platform to promote social change.*

Miss Marie Tempest: A whirlwind of energy and talent, she captivates audiences with her dynamic stage presence and her sparkling voice. Her performances are a testament to her versatility and her ability to command attention. *Tempest's career spanned both light opera and legitimate theatre, demonstrating her range* *and ability to adapt to different genres.*

Miss Fay Templeton: A comedic force of nature, she's a master of improvisation and a born scene-stealer. Her performances are full of unexpected twists and turns, leaving audiences both delighted and slightly bewildered by her untamed talent. *Templeton's comedic talent was so renowned that she was often compared to male comedic stars of the day, breaking down gender barriers in the field of comedy.*

(And Many Other Unique and Compelling Performers of the American Stage)

Note: This cast of characters highlights a relevant or interesting fact about each performer that connects them to the present day, either through their lasting legacy, their pioneering spirit, or their impact on the entertainment industry. It aims to show that these women were not just talented performers but also individuals who shaped the world around them.

From Footlights to Followers: The Prima Donna and the Social Media Influencer

Though separated by a century of technological and cultural shifts, the prima donnas of the late 19th and early 20th centuries share surprising similarities with the social media influencers of today. Both groups have cultivated devoted followings, built personal brands, and wielded considerable influence over popular culture, albeit through vastly different mediums. By examining these parallels, we can gain a deeper appreciation for the enduring power of personality and performance in shaping public perception and driving trends.

One striking similarity lies in the cultivation of a devoted following. The prima donnas, with their captivating stage presence and magnetic personalities, commanded the adoration of theatergoers who eagerly awaited their every performance. Similarly, social media influencers, through carefully curated content and engaging interactions, amass vast numbers of followers who eagerly consume their every post and video. Both groups understand the importance of building a loyal audience and fostering a sense of connection with their fans, whether through stage door encounters or live Q&A sessions on Instagram.

Both prima donnas and influencers are masters of personal branding. The prima donnas cultivated distinct stage personas, emphasizing their unique talents and personalities to stand out in a crowded field. Lillian Russell's glamorous image, Edna May's innocent charm, and Marie Dressler's boisterous humor were all carefully constructed brands that resonated with specific audiences. Likewise, social media influencers meticulously craft their online personas, showcasing their expertise, lifestyle, or unique point of view to attract a dedicated following. Whether it's a fashion blogger's impeccable style, a fitness guru's motivational message, or a comedian's relatable humor, personal branding is crucial for success in both spheres.

The influence wielded by prima donnas and influencers extends beyond mere entertainment. The prima donnas, with their immense popularity, set fashion trends, endorsed products, and even influenced social and political discourse. Lillian Russell's embrace of cycling helped popularize the activity for women, while Edna May's "Gibson Girl" look became a fashion sensation. Similarly, social media influencers can drive consumer behavior, promote social causes, and even sway political opinions. Fashion influencers can launch new trends with a single post, while activists can raise awareness for important issues through viral campaigns. The power of both groups lies in their ability to connect with their audience on a personal level and inspire action.

However, it's important to acknowledge the key differences between these two groups. The prima donnas primarily relied on live performance and limited media exposure, while influencers leverage the immediacy and reach of the internet. The level of control over their image and message also differs significantly, with influencers having greater autonomy in shaping their online narrative.

Despite these differences, the parallels between prima donnas and social media influencers reveal the enduring appeal of personality-driven entertainment and the power of individuals to shape popular culture. Both groups demonstrate that success hinges on cultivating a devoted following, building a strong personal brand, and wielding influence responsibly. As we navigate the ever-evolving landscape of entertainment and media, understanding the lessons of the past can offer valuable insights into the dynamics of influence and the enduring power of performance, whether on the stage or on the screen.

Browsable Glossary

Double entendre This is one of those phrases that sound very fancy, but, you know, the French just love to be suggestive. They can't help themselves.

Embonpoint This is a fancy way of saying "fat." But let's be honest, it's the kind of fat that makes you think of "ample" and "comfortable," not "grossly notorious."

Extra girl This refers to a woman in the chorus, or, you know, one of the dancers. Usually a "girl" in a chorus is someone who's only there for the scenery–and the scenery is probably better.

Faience This is a French term, very fancy, that just means pottery. Why would anyone even mention it? As if it's something terribly important. It's just pottery.

Floria This word really just means "flowery," which is

how they describe some kinds of music. It's not that different from "flowery language."

Fortissimo This is an Italian term, also fancy, that means really loud. It's what people in the chorus do.

Gallic This is a fancy way of saying French, though let's be honest, no one in the book is truly French–they're all just sort of trying to sound like it.

Gag This word has lost a lot of its charm since the turn of the century. It just means a funny line or a silly action that actors use to get a laugh. A lot of these gags are old and tired.

German This is a general word for all things German–which is about as accurate as calling everything American "Yankee." It's too broad.

Greasepaint This is what actors use on their faces to make themselves look different. But it's not exactly makeup–it's much more obvious and sometimes just plain ugly.

Grisette This word refers to a French working-class woman, especially a seamstress, but the way people use it in the book makes you think it's just another way of saying "prostitute." They're always describing the French as being so very "suggestive."

Hodge-podge This means "a mixture of different things." But it's not exactly a salad–it's more like a soup made of whatever happens to be on hand.

Ingenue This refers to a naive, innocent young woman–usually played by a young woman who's not naive or innocent at all.

Interpolated This is a fancy way of saying "stuck in." The book is full of "interpolated" songs, which just means that they weren't part of the original score but were added in later.

Irish The way people describe the Irish in this book is just plain offensive. They're like caricatures, not real people.

Italians The book doesn't really talk about Italian people, but if they did, I'm sure they'd make a big deal out of the fact that they were Italians. After all, they're all about making everything sound grand and romantic.

Jumping-jack fashion This just means a funny kind of dance. You know, like a jumping jack.

Lay figure This is a fancy way of saying "a doll." The book uses the phrase to describe the way some women act in opera–they're just standing around like they're not even real.

Legitimate This is a word that actors use to describe plays that are not musicals. But sometimes it's just a way of saying that the play is boring.

Libretto This is a fancy word for the text of an opera. But they really just mean the story.

Limelight This is a word that means "fame" or "popularity." It comes from the old days when they used a special kind of lamp to shine a bright light on the actors.

Low comedy This is a kind of comedy that's really silly and makes fun of ordinary people. It's not exactly sophisticated.

Mascot This is a lucky charm, or, you know, someone who's supposed to bring good luck. People in this book are obsessed with their mascots, as if it's something real and powerful.

Metronome This is a device that musicians use to keep time. But the book says that John Philip Sousa keeps a metronome "clacking" at his elbow as he writes. It's a funny image, but it also makes you think that his music is really too mechanical.

Midshipmate This is a word that refers to a sailor. They really mean "a little boy" who's dressed as a sailor.

Minstrel This word refers to a type of entertainment that was popular in the 19th century. It usually involved blackface makeup and stereotyped characters.

Musical comedy This is a kind of play that has music and dancing. But the book is really more about the women than about the actual music.

Music-hall This refers to a kind of theatre that was popular in England in the 19th century. It usually featured variety acts, such as singers, dancers, and comedians.

Naivete This is a fancy word for "innocence" or "simplicity." It's a quality that people in the book are always talking about, even though the women they're describing are not really all that innocent. They're just playing the part.

Olio This is a word that means "a mixture of different things." It's like a potluck, or a mixed salad. But in the book, it's usually used to describe a variety show.

Opera The word is Italian for "work" and refers to a kind of play with music and singing.

Opera Comique This is a French term for a type of opera that is light and humorous. But again, it's mostly about the women.

Operetta This is a short opera. The book often uses the words "operetta" and "opera" interchangeably.

Pantomime This is a kind of acting without words. It's about using your body to tell a story. Sometimes it's really obvious and sometimes it's really subtle.

Parisian The book is full of words like this. But it's just a way of saying "fancy" or "sophisticated." People in the book think that anything French is inherently better than anything American.

Pathetic This is a word that means "sad" or "pitiful." The book loves to describe the women in opera as "pathetic," as if they're not strong enough to handle the pressure of being on stage.

Pate-de-foie gras The book uses this word to describe Marie Tempest, as if she were some kind of delicacy.

Performers This word is just another way of saying "actors." But it's a little less fancy.

Personality This is the key to the whole book. The author is obsessed with personality, which is what he thinks makes these women so successful. But personality is a very slippery thing–you can't really define it, you just have to feel it.

Prima donna This is the lead female singer in an opera. But the book uses the term for any woman in opera.

Prince The book has a lot of women who are playing princes or men disguised as princes. It's sort of a convention of opera.

Prudish modesty This is a way of describing women who are very modest and proper. The book uses it to describe women in opera, as if they're all like that in real life.

Quizzical squint This is a way of describing a person who's looking at you in a funny way, with one eyebrow raised. The book uses it to describe a character who's mischievous.

Rhapsodies This is a word that means "exciting stories." It's a way of describing the way people talk about opera, as if it were some kind of magical art form.

Ringer-in This is a way of saying "something that's been added in to make things look better." The book uses the term to describe the plot of a Sousa opera–the music is catchy, but the story is not very interesting.

Roman chariot This is a kind of horse-drawn carriage that was used by the Romans. The book uses it to describe the kind of vehicle that Pauline Hall drove in a circus-like show.

Romanza This is an Italian word that means "romance." But in this book, it's just a song.

Roof gardens This is a kind of outdoor entertainment venue that was popular in the late 19th century. It usually featured variety acts and dancing.

Royal good fellow This is a way of describing someone who is kind and friendly. The book uses it to describe Marie Dressler, even though she's a comedian.

Sabots These are wooden shoes that were worn by peasants in the Netherlands. The book uses this word to describe a woman's shoes in a Dutch character sketch.

Salvation Army This is a religious organization that helps people in need. The book uses it to describe the kind of women that Edna May played on stage.

Satire This is a kind of humor that makes fun of someone or something. The book uses it to describe a way of acting that is subtle and clever.

Soubrette This is a kind of actress who is usually young and pretty and plays a mischievous or flirtatious character. It's not a very important role, but it's always fun to watch.

Spectacular This is a kind of play that is mostly about the scenery and the special effects.

Stage business This is the way that actors move around and interact with each other on stage. It's not exactly acting, but it's important to create a good impression.

Statuesque This is a fancy word for "tall and beautiful." It's a word that's often used to describe women in opera.

Stool This is a kind of chair without a back. It's what people used to sit on before they had fancy chairs.

Street parade This is a parade that goes through the streets of a city. The book uses it to describe a parade that was part of a circus-like show.

Swedish Nightingale This is a famous nickname for Jenny Lind, a Swedish singer who was popular in the 19th century. But the book uses it as a way of mocking a singer who's not very good.

Swell This is a word that means "fashionable" or "stylish." The book uses it to describe the way that some people dress and act.

Take-off This is a way of saying "a parody" or "an imitation." It's a way of making fun of someone or something by copying them.

Tenor This is the high male voice in an opera.

Terpsichorean This is a fancy word for "dancing."

Tights This is what women wear on their legs when they're playing boys' parts in opera.

Topical song This is a song that's about something that's happening in the news. It's a kind of song that's popular with comedians.

Travesty This is a word that means "a parody" or "an imitation." It's usually used to describe something that is ridiculous.

Triple alliance This is a group of three people or things that are working together. The book uses the term to describe a group of three opera stars.

Troupe This is a group of actors or singers. It's sort of like a team.

Tunic This is a kind of shirt that was worn by men in the ancient world. It's often worn by women in opera when they're playing boys' parts.

Twickenham Ferry This is the name of a song. You know, one of those old-fashioned songs.

Variety This is a kind of entertainment that features different acts, such as singers, dancers, and comedians.

Variety sketch This is a short play that's usually funny and involves a few characters.

Vaudeville This is a kind of entertainment that features a mix of variety acts. It's sort of like a variety show, but it's more elaborate.

Venus This is the Roman goddess of love and beauty.

Viennese This is a word that means "from Vienna," which is a city in Austria. But in this book, it's just a way of saying "fancy" or "sophisticated."

Vivacity This is a word that means "lively" or "energetic." It's a quality that a lot of women in the book have.

Vocal gymnastics This is a fancy way of saying "singing really hard."

Witch-finder-general This is a person who was appointed by the king to find and punish witches. It's a very old-fashioned job.

Womanish This is a way of describing a woman who's acting like a man, but in a silly way. It's not a flattering term.

Womanly This is a way of describing a woman who is feminine and graceful.

Yankee This is an old-fashioned word for an American, though it's usually used to describe someone from the North.

Yum Yum This is the name of a character in the Gilbert and Sullivan opera "The Mikado." It's a very silly name.

Timeline

1856 - Charles E. Leonard issues the first number of the "Clinton Herald," in Clinton, Iowa.

1861 - Lillian Russell (née Helen Louise Leonard) is born in Clinton, Iowa.

1865 - Charles E. Leonard moves the job office connected with the "Clinton Herald" to Chicago.

1866 - Jessie Bartlett Davis is born in Morris, Illinois.

1872 - Della Fox is born in St. Louis.

1874 - Lulu Glaser is born in Allegheny City, Pennsylvania.

1875 - Minnie Ashley (née Minnie Whitehead) performs at children's festivals in Boston, Massachusetts.

1875 - Pauline Hall makes her first stage appearance in the chorus of Robinson's Opera House in Cincinnati.

1877 - Camille D'Arville makes her first appearance in concert in Amsterdam.

1880 - Pauline Hall joins Edward E. Rice's "Surprise Party" and begins her professional acting career.

1881 - Pauline Hall marries Edward White in St. Louis, Missouri.

1882 - Josephine Hall makes her professional debut as Eulalie in "Evangeline" at the Fourteenth Street Theatre, New York City.

1883 - Camille D'Arville makes her professional debut in the operetta "Cymbria, or the Magic Thimble" at the Strand Theatre, London.

1883 - Pauline Hall creates the part of Venus in "Orpheus and Eurydice" at the Bijou Opera House, New York City.

1885 - Camille D'Arville stars in "Chilperic" at the Empire Theatre, London.

1886 - Marie Tempest makes her stage debut in "Boccaccio" at the London Comedy Theatre.

1886 - Jessie Bartlett Davis studies in Paris, France.

1887 - Virginia Earle makes her stage debut as Nanki

Poo in "The Mikado" with the Home Juvenile Opera Company.

1887 - Marie Tempest stars in "Dorothy" at the Prince of Wales Theatre, London.

1888 - Lillian Russell makes her first appearance as the Princess in "Nadjy" at the New York Casino.

1888 - Camille D'Arville stars in "Rip Van Winkle" at the Empire Theatre, London.

1888 - Lillian Russell stars in "The Brigands" at the New York Casino.

1890 - Della Fox stars in "Castles in the Air" at the Broadway Theatre, New York City.

1890 - Marie Celeste makes her stage debut in "The Great Metropolis" at the Halifax Theatre, Nova Scotia.

1890 - Fay Templeton stars in "Hendrik Hudson" at the Fourteenth Street Theatre, New York City.

1891 - Edna Wallace Hopper makes her stage debut as Mabel Douglass in "The Club Friend" at the Boston Museum.

1891 - Della Fox stars in "Wang" at the Broadway Theatre, New York City.

1892 - Alice Nielsen makes her stage debut as Yum Yum in "The Mikado" with the Pike Opera Company.

1892 - Pauline Hall stars in "Puritania" at the Boston Museum.

1892 - Christie MacDonald joins Francis Wilson's company and makes her stage debut in "The Lion Tamer" at the Broadway Theatre, New York City.

1893 - Edna Wallace Hopper marries DeWolf Hopper.

1893 - Camille D'Arville stars in "Venus" at the Boston Museum.

1893 - Marie Tempest makes her first appearance at the New York Casino as the successor to Lillian Russell and Pauline Hall.

1893 - Marie Tempest stars in "The Fencing Master" in New York City.

1894 - Lillian Russell marries Giovanni Perugini (John Chatterton).

1894 - Della Fox makes her debut as a star in "The Little Trooper" at the New York Casino.

1895 - Jessie Bartlett Davis joins the American Opera Company.

1895 - Josephine Hall stars in "Mam'selle 'Awkins" at the Fourteenth Street Theatre, New York City.

1895 - Hilda Clark makes her stage debut as the Princess Bonnie in "The Princess Bonnie".

1896 - Edna Wallace Hopper stars in "El Capitan" at the Boston Museum.

1897 - Josephine Hall stars in "The Girl from Paris" at the Fourteenth Street Theatre, New York City.

1897 - Della Fox stars in "The Wedding Day" at the New York Casino.

1898 - Alice Nielsen makes her debut as a star in "The Fortune Teller" at the New York Casino.

1898 - Lulu Glaser makes her stage debut as a star in "The Merry Monarch" at the New York Casino.

1898 - Maud Raymond joins the Rogers Brothers company.

1899 - Fay Templeton joins the Weber and Fields Company.

1899 - Minnie Ashley stars in "The Chorus Girl" at the Boston Museum.

1900 - Edna May stars in "The Belle of New York" in New York City.

1900 - Mabelle Gilman stars in "The Rounders" at the New York Casino.

1900 - Christie MacDonald stars in "The Princess Chic" at the Columbia Theatre, Boston.

1900 - Paula Edwardes stars in "Mam'selle 'Awkins" at the Fourteenth Street Theatre, New York City.

Milton Keynes UK
Ingram Content Group UK Ltd.
UKHW020831151024
449705UK00017B/581